Letterland

16 pages

Early Years Workbook 4

Letters: t-z

Name:

Find Talking Tess's letters on the tortoise. Make each of her letters brown.

Write Talking Tess's letter here.

Find the toys in the trunk that begin with Talking Tess's sound. Then colour them.

Draw something that begins with my sound.

Find Uppy Umbrella's letters on the big umbrella. Make them blue.

Write Uppy Umbrella's letter here.

Make the two things you can go up in red. Make the two things you can go under blue.

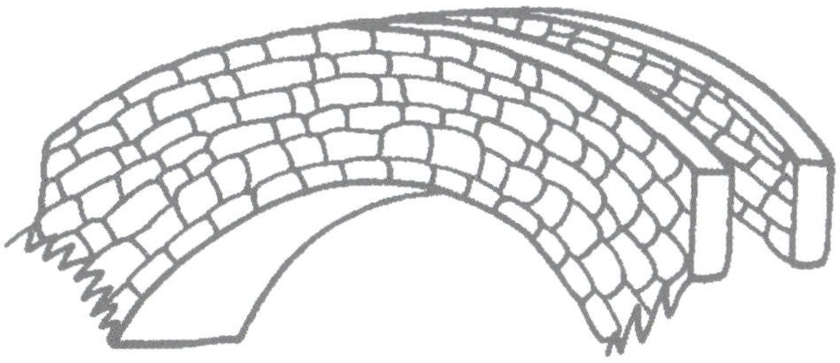

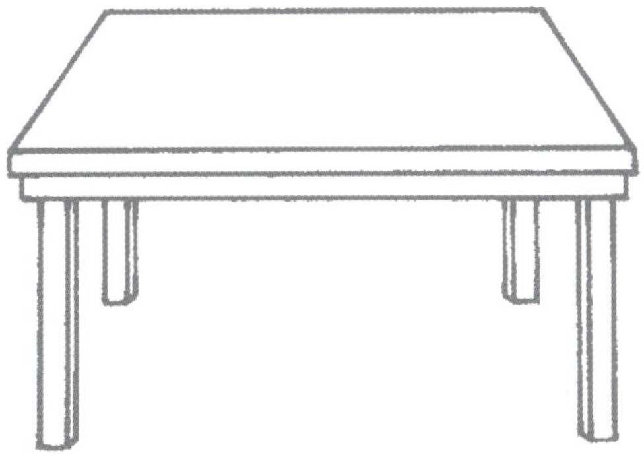

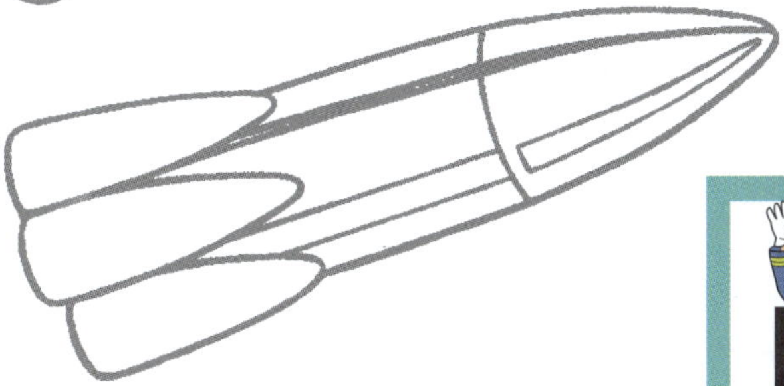

Sometimes I say my name in words. Say my rhyme and see!

This horse with a horn is called a unicorn.

Find Vicky Violet's letters on the side of the van. Make them purple.

Write Vicky Violet's letter here.

Circle the things that begin with Vicky Violet's sound.

Can you draw five different vegetables?

Find Walter Walrus's letters in the spider's web. Make them blue.

Write Walter Walrus's letter here.

Join the dots to find out what Walter Walrus would like for his birthday.

If you could make a wish, what would you wish for? Draw it.

Find Fix-it Max's letters on the big birthday card. Make them red.

Happy Birthday

X X
X W

Write Fix-it Max's letter here.

10

Find the pictures with Fix-it Max's sound in them. Circle them.

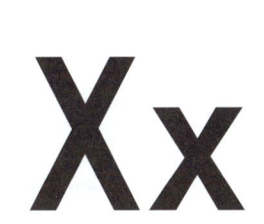

6

What do you think is in the box? Can you draw it here?

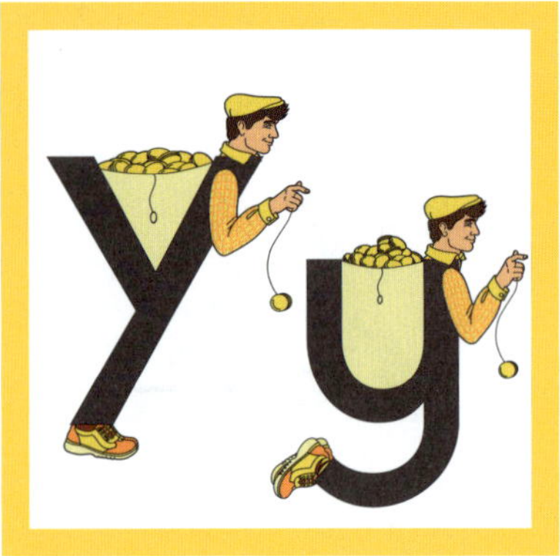

Find the Yellow Yo-yo Man's letters. Make them yellow.

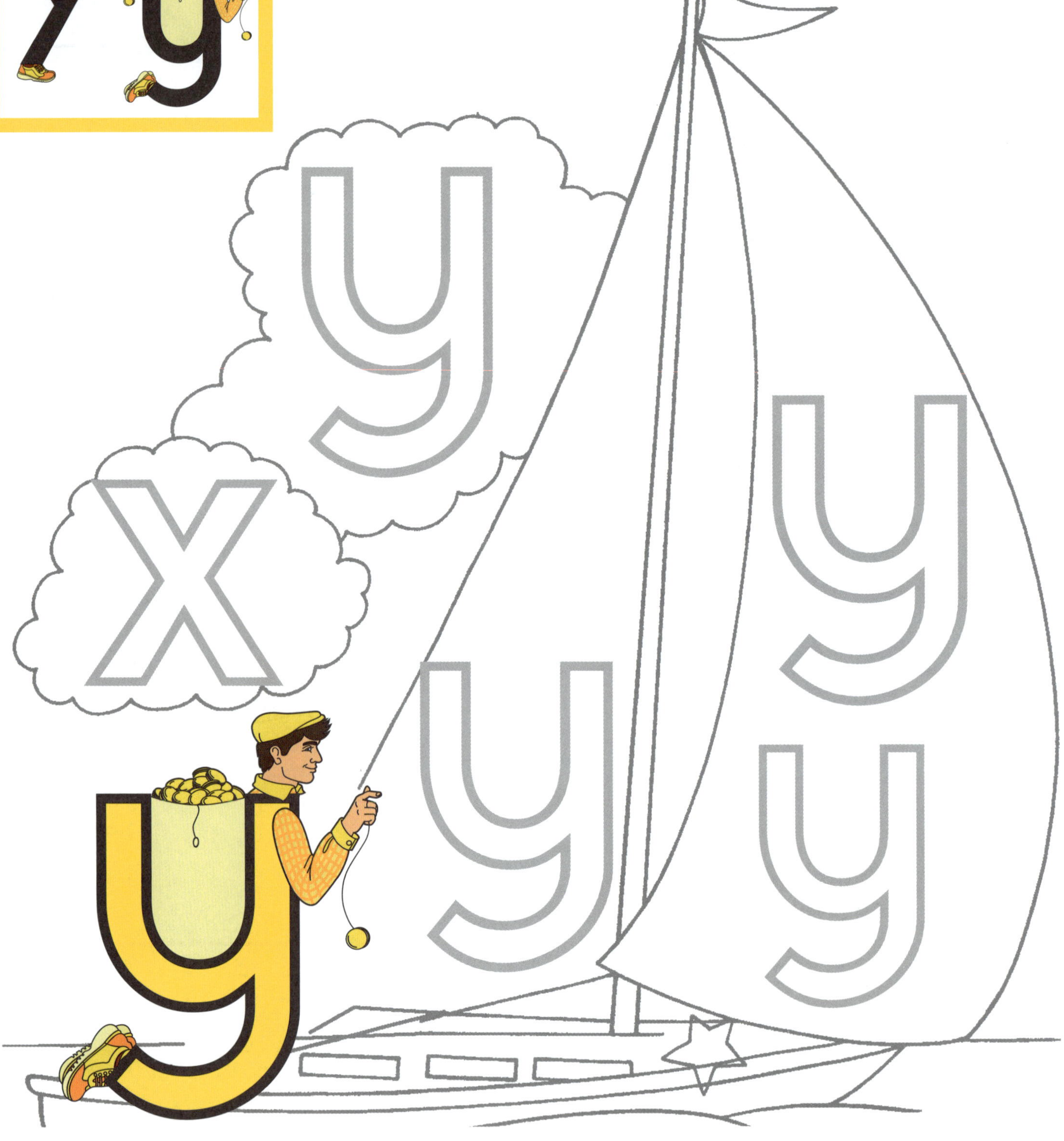

Write Yellow Yo-yo Man's letter here.

Find the things that begin with Yellow Yo-yo Man's sound.
Join them to the Yo-yo Man.

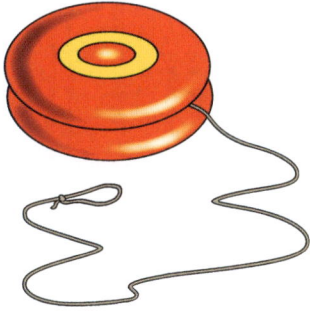

Draw a picture of something that you did yesterday.

Find Zig Zag Zebra's letters and colour them.

Write Zig Zag Zebra's letter here.

Which pictures begin with Zig Zag Zebra's sound? Draw zig zag lines to her letter.

 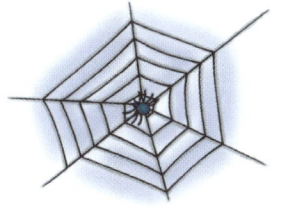 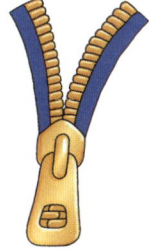 

Z   W   Z   Z

Draw some animals for the Letterland zoo.

Look at the names under each picture. Then draw the Letterlander.

Talking Tess

Uppy Umbrella

Vicky Violet

Walter Walrus

Fix-it Max

Yellow Yo-yo Man

Zig Zag Zebra

Published by Letterland International Ltd,
8/10 South Street, Epsom, Surrey, KT18 7PF, UK
© Letterland International 2006
ISBN: 978-1-86209-352-2

First published 1997.
This revised edition published 2006.
Reprinted 2008, 2011, 2012, 2014, 2018,
2020, 2021, 2023.
18 17 16 15 14

LETTERLAND™ is a trademark of Letterland International Ltd.

Written by Louis Fidge
Illustrated by Anna Jupp and Kathy Baxendale
Consultant: Lyn Wendon, originator of Letterland

All rights reserved. No part of this publication may be reproduced, stored in a retrieval system, or transmitted in any form or by any means, electronic, mechanical, photocopying, recording or otherwise, without the prior permission of the Publisher or a licence permitting restricted copying in the United Kingdom issued by the Copyright Licensing Agency Ltd, 90 Tottenham Court Road, London W1P 0LP.

British Library Cataloguing in Publication Data. A catalogue record for this book is available from the British Library.

Printed in Guangdong Province, China.

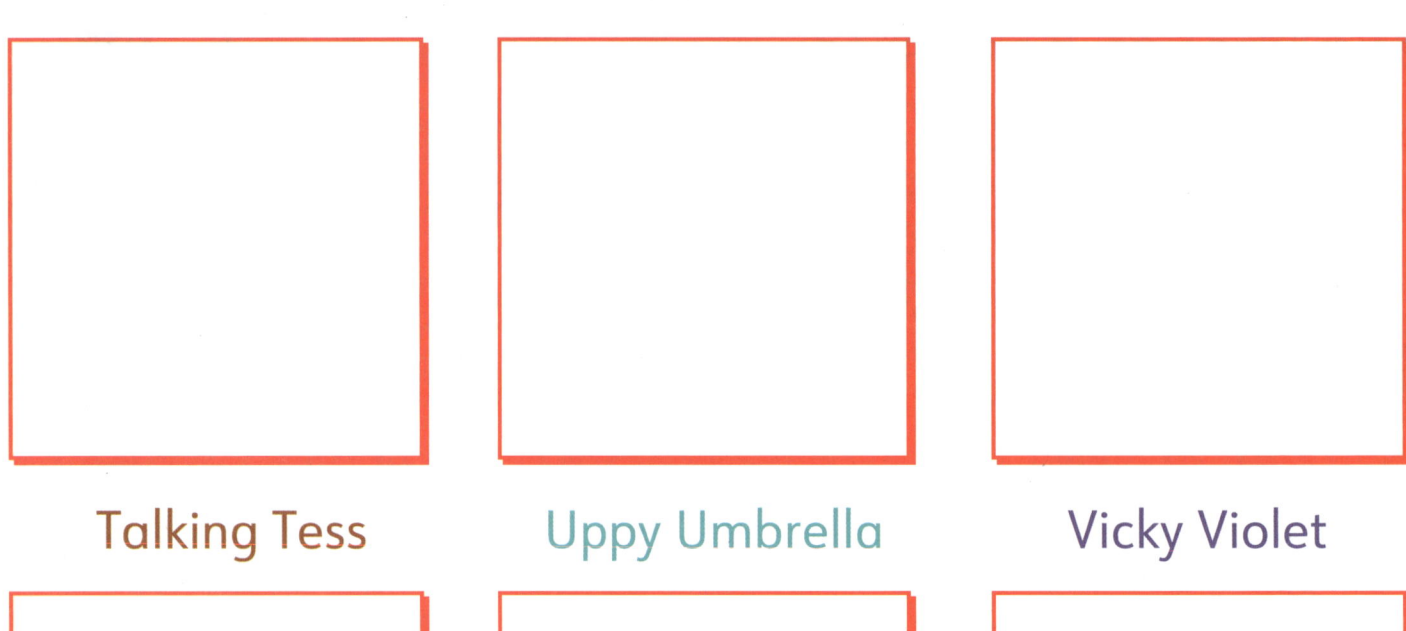

Code: T62
ISBN 978-1-86209-352-2
9 781862 093522